ARCHES
&
CANYONLANDS
NATIONAL PARKS

It is a lovely and terrible wilderness...
harshly and beautifully colored,
broken and worn until its bones are exposed...
in hidden corners and pockets under the cliffs
the sudden poetry of springs.

Wallace Stegner, *The Sound of Mountain Water*, 1969

POCKET PORTFOLIO®
–Number One–

ARCHES
&
CANYONLANDS

NATIONAL PARKS

including
WALKING in CANYON COUNTRY
by
NICKY LEACH

SIERRA PRESS
Mariposa, CA

Riparian habitat along Courthouse Wash, summer, Arches National Park.

We would like to thank Brad Wallis, Nancy Gebhardt, and Sharon Brussel of Canyonlands Natural History Association, Diane Allen of Arches National Park, as well as Bruce Rogers and Nancy Coulam of Canyonlands National Park for their assistance in the creation of this book. We would also like to take this opportunity to thank the many photographers who made their imagery available to us during the editing of this title—Thank You!

ISBN O-939365-53-7

Printed in Singapore. First Edition: Spring 1997. Second printing: Spring 2002.
Third Printing: Spring 2005. Fourth Printing: Spring 2007.

Front Cover: Delicate Arch, late afternoon, Arches N.P.
Frontispiece: Handprint pictographs, Canyonlands N.P.
Title Page: The La Sal Mountains seen through Mesa Arch, sunset,
          Island in the Sky District, Canyonlands N.P.
Back Cover: Rainbow over Grays Pasture, Island in the Sky,
Canyonlands N.P.

NOTE TO THE READER:
          The term "ancestral Pueblo" in this book refers
          to the culture formerly known as Anasazi.

The La Sal Mountains and rainbow seen from The Neck, Island in the Sky District, Canyonlands National Park.

Living with an elevation range of between 4,000 and 6,000 feet, eight inches of annual rainfall, torrid summers, and frigid winters, plants and animals have to be tough customers to make it here. Atop the plateaus and in areas with deeper soils, pinyon-juniper woodlands and native galleta grass and Indian ricegrass take hold, while old man sage and scrub oak occupy dune areas. Blackbrush, with its preference for gravelly sections, dominates much of the land. Pricklypear and other cactus occupy arid lowlands, but you'll find only salt-tolerant pickleweed and seepweed in Arches' salt valleys. The land is mainly slickrock and sand, incapable of retaining moisture from a passing thundercloud, so wildlife gravitates toward rivers and springs, and to potholes filled with rainwater. The acid green of cottonwoods and brilliant scarlet of monkeyflower are reminders that water is a precious commodity here in the desert.

Sandstone landscape at dusk seen from Anticline Overlook, Canyon Rims Recreation Area (BLM).

Until recently, Utah's remote canyonlands remained inaccessible and largely unknown. Ute and Paiute Indians succeeded departed ancestral Puebloans in the canyons, then, throughout the nineteenth century, a few fur trappers, miners, Mormon settlers, ranchers, outlaws, and adventurers wandered into the region. Government expeditions explored the newly acquired United States territory in the mid-1800s, the most famous of which were Major John Wesley Powell's two explorations of the Green and Colorado Rivers. But other than marveling at the unearthly scenery, no one could know that a uranium boom and recreation would eventually attract thousands here. In 1859, geologist John Strong Newberry of the Macomb expedition was particularly dismissive, writing: "I cannot conceive of a more worthless and impracticable region than the one we now found ourselves in."

Buttes, mesas, and the Green River—stormy afternoon seen from Island in the Sky, Canyonlands National Park.

WALKING IN CANYON COUNTRY, I KEEP MY EYES ON MY FEET. Cairns offer subtle clues for me to follow. But mostly I go on instinct, placing one foot in front of the other, heel to toe. Walking meditation in a Zen rock garden. My breathing slows. I listen for rustling in the bushes, pay attention to far-off thunder and rain on the breeze, stay out of washes in summertime.

This is how I am in this place: quiet, attentive, slow, rhythmic, goal-less. My reward is simply that I am here.

At knee level, a whole world is waiting to be discovered. Feathery old man sage. Prickly blackbrush. Bleached jawbones of stripped juniper. Furry coyote scat. A pale *mariposa* resting on a scarlet globemallow. Biting red ants scurry about, cleaning up the desert. Cheeks bulging with seeds, a ground squirrel, feather duster tail held aloft, caches a winter larder among the protected roots of a dwarf pine. A jackrabbit hops in front of me. I can see the blood coursing through its large jackass ears, cooling an overheated body. Overhead, a kestrel is circling the sky looking for a deer mouse for breakfast. These residents don't mind my presence. They go about their business as I go about mine. Their lack of interest fills me with an inexplicable joy.

Sandstone silhouettes at Klondike Bluffs, Arches National Park.

Composed of horizontal beds of sedimentary rocks, the landscape seems to be all planes and curves. To understand its scale and transmuted nature, you must travel among the narrow canyons and the towering landforms and look up. The rivers have incised pathways 2,000 feet deep through what was once nearly a mile of horizontal rocks sitting atop unstable, 300 million-year-old basement salt deposits. The rimrock here—the Navajo Sandstone—is already 175 million years old. What happened to 125 million years of geologic history? Remnants can be seen in the eroded Entrada landforms of Arches National Park, in the fossil-rich cliffs of the Morrison Formation to the north, and in the igneous rocks of the surrounding mountains. The rest, as they say, is history.

Hikers in the depths of the Joint Trail, Needles District, Canyonlands National Park.

Reflection of Angel Arch in Salt Creek, Canyonlands National Park.

My route skirts hillocks of dark cryptobiotic crust, the texture of brown sugar. Life teems here, within a delicate triumvirate of cyanobacteria, lichen, and algae that helps stop the desert blowing away, attracts moisture, and creates new soil. These ancient biological alliances may already be a hundred years old. I walk carefully and tip my cap to the microbial elders all around me. Their survival is as important as mine. We are all in this together.

Every few minutes, I stop to drink water and scan the fiery sandstone cliffs tilting toward the northwestern horizon. Fingers of cracked sandstone evolve into fins, then fall into a corps of oddly eroded, streaked monoliths known as the Marching Men. Five tall officers with rifles, a junior sergeant bringing up the rear. Deep crevices hold moist sand, a livid green single-leaf ash, an arthritic bonsai juniper, a hidden falcon's nest. The tiny movements of plants and animals dislodge a pebble here, a shower of sand there.

A mound of claret cup cactus in bloom.

Water and ice enter the rocks, weaken the cemented grains, and widen the crevices into slabs that resemble dominoes. The Entrada and Navajo Sandstone will shear along fractures, spall into alcoves and arches, narrow into freestanding towers and balanced rocks, then tumble into memory. Fiery Furnace, Landscape Arch, Balanced Rock, the Windows, Park Avenue, Skyline Arch. All will have their turn on stage in this ancient amphitheater, their rise and fall orchestrated by the triple impresarios of moving underground salt, restless earth movements, and fickle weather. The spotlight will fade. The land will transform. New landmarks will appear.

High among the boulders and straight cliffs, I come upon fresh tracks: a mule deer's elegant heart-shaped hoofprints and the large, fist-sized paw prints of a mountain lion loping back and forth between high ledge and dense cover. Hunter and prey. Sacrifice and Life. The silence deepens. My heart beats faster. I can hear the blood rushing in my ears. I feel cougar eyes watching me.

Even the barest, most inhospitable sections of Canyonlands and Arches support life. Autumn-hued lichens cluster atop rocks and gradually break down their hosts through acidic excretions until pockets of moist soil form—the perfect spot for a thrifty pinyon or juniper. Sandy areas have their own benefactor. Dark, crumbly patches of cryptobiotic soil blanket the landscape and form strange hillocks that look like mole hills. They are actually a complex living mixture of cyanobacteria, lichens, mosses, algae, and fungi, which form fibers that anchor soil, retain water, and decrease erosion and runoff. Once established, desert plants offer essential food and shelter to animals, including humans. Watch where you walk. Walk only in sandy washes, on slickrock, or on the trails. In the desert, nature's bonds are fragile and easily broken.

Cryptobiotic soil and Wooden Shoe Arch near Squaw Flat, Needles District, Canyonlands National Park.

Queen Nefertiti, Park Avenue area, Arches National Park.

Inside Double Arch, Windows area, Arches National Park.

Sweating from the walled-in heat and primitive excitement, I move quickly through the narrow pass. Tower Arch lies just ahead, its enormous opening of glowing rose sandstone set back among its kind. Beside the span is a tall column protected by a smooth helmet of pale caprock. Swelling stone lips mark the entrance to the inner sanctum. A peaceful feeling floods over me. I lean back into a warm curve of slickrock, my eyes resting dreamily on the contours of the arch. I crush fragrant sage between forefinger and thumb and map my immigrant route into this country with a fingernail, inscribing concentric circles and wavy lines into rough stone. I am no longer foreign. I cannot tell the difference between my flesh and the skin of stone covering the bones of the earth beneath me. Everything seems conscious, intentional, sweeping me along with it. Eros is alive in these portals. I walk through, entranced.

Monument Basin seen from the White Rim, Canyonlands National Park.

The predominant rocks of Canyon Country are rainbow-hued Entrada, Navajo, White Rim, Wingate, and Cedar Mesa sandstones. Percolating groundwater, fracturing, and erosion cause porous sandstones to shear into cliffs, fins, alcoves, arches, and other epic landforms. Springs, seeps, and waterfalls emerge at the base of cliffs, where sandstone meets narrow ledges of water-tight shales, siltstones, and mudstones. The springlines soon foster lush hanging gardens of fern, columbine, monkeyflower, and other water-loving plants, but the dripping undermines the cliffs above, leading to their collapse. The thick Pennsylvanian-era Paradox Formation salt deposits that move uneasily around the basement of the region can be seen occasionally at river level, where they appear pale, crumbly, and misleadingly benign.

Skyline Arch, winter sunset in Devils Garden, Arches National Park.

Arches became a national monument by presidential proclamation in 1929. It was upgraded to congression-
ally approved national park status under President Nixon in 1971. Today the park covers 114 square miles, but
the original proposed scenic area was in the northwestern section of the park, in the area of Klondike Bluffs,
the site of a mining claim worked by a German immigrant named Ringhoffer and his family in 1922.
Ringhoffer interested railroad officials in the scenic possibilities of the area and even proposed the name
Devils Garden for it—a name that was eventually shifted to another section of Arches. Although the rail route
did not end up crossing nearby, the sandstone treasures of Arches are now known to millions worldwide.

Landscape Arch at sunrise, Devils Garden, Arches National Park.

"LIFE IS A SPELL SO EXQUISITE THAT EVERYTHING CONSPIRES TO BREAK IT," writes Emily Dickinson. Ah, to place ourselves under the spell of this timeless landscape. To let go of human conquest, our reasoning mind, and simply step into our animal dreams.

I feel enchantment in Arches National Park, in this giant's playroom crammed with bizarre clay sculptures left to bake in the sun. Bald-pated "Old Man" Tukuhnikivats, one of the loftiest of the La Sal peaks, watches benignly from his 12,000-foot perch. Sunlight and shadow dodge over the hoodoos and windows of rock that sit at his feet. Solitary Delicate Arch moves closer to the precipice. Elegant Landscape Arch becomes ever more svelte. The maze of passageways in the Fiery Furnace beckon. What are the Three Gossips saying?

La Sal Mountains seen through Delicate Arch, Arches National Park.

In a landscape such as this, we are invited into a primal relationship with nature. In wonder, we touch, taste, smell, walk around the strange rocks, look at them from all angles, try to get close enough to learn something. The arches draw us magnetically to them. Then our minds say, "Okay. That's enough. There are other places to get to." Why do we resist walking in the wild? What are we afraid of? "Been there. Done that," we shrug. We measure the speed at which we can get from here to there, walk swiftly, longing for the thrill of attainment, possession. Are we brave enough to allow ourselves to be possessed instead?

Sunset in the Garden of Eden (aerial view), Arches National Park.

Arches proliferate in Arches National Park (more than 2,000 at last count) due to very deep salt deposits beneath the Paradox Basin. Salt liquefies and flows away from heavy overlying rocks until ancient fault blocks intervene and it is forced to dome upward. Groundwater enters fractures in these salt-intruded domes, or anticlines, and dissolves the salt, helping to create a series of parallel rock "fins" along fault lines in the Entrada and Navajo Sandstone. Once exposed, the fins are sculpted by erosion into arches, spires, and balanced rocks. Collapsing due to salt dissolution is dramatic. Delicate Arch sits right on the lip of Salt Valley, while along the Moab Fault, near the visitor center, strata on one side of the valley are 2,500 feet higher than the other.

Stormy morning light on The Organ, Courthouse Towers area, Arches National Park.

Ironically, it is the desert's most precious resource—water—that is responsible for the look of the land. Silty river waters and roaring late-summer flashfloods carve narrow, winding canyons here, while rainfall, ice, and snow are the primary sculptors of the buttes, benches, monoliths, arches, and bizarre hoodoos that spark the imagination. Their odd appearance is the result of differential erosion, whereby strata of assorted compositions, hardnesses, and thicknesses erode at different rates and in distinctive ways. This gradual process is rarely seen but can result in dramatic rockfalls. In 1940, for example, an eroding boulder fell away from Skyline Arch and doubled the size of the arch overnight. Similar rockfalls have thinned Landscape Arch more recently.

Balanced Rock and rising moon, Arches National Park.

Small arch in the Windows area, Arches National Park.

My friend Scott once swore he heard "the geological tick of time" among the arches during a September rainstorm. Perhaps these fantastic rocks are icons, symbols of something we can't quite remember in our subconscious—remnants of the original Garden. The great mythologist Joseph Campbell thought that what human beings are looking for is "an experience of living," not "the meaning of life." If that is what we want, why is it so hard to sit quietly and let this place whisper its story, for us to recount our own? Have we forgotten how to enter sacred places?

Utah juniper precariously perched at Green River Overlook, Island in the Sky District, Canyonlands National Park.

Canyonlands National Park covers 527 square miles and is split into the Island in the Sky, Needles, Maze, and River Districts. It's hard country to get around in—but remoteness is one of its greatest attractions. The park was established in 1964, through the efforts of Arches National Park Superintendent Bates Wilson and then Secretary of the Interior Stewart Udall. Wilson, a true lover of Canyon Country, became the park's first superintendent. Don't expect to see the whole park in one go. Each district is a long way from the others and has its own unique features. You'll need a lifetime to see the whole thing. Choose one section, buy a good topo map, plenty of supplies, and then explore the many foot trails and four-wheel-drive roads.

Early morning at Grandview Point, Island in the Sky District, Canyonlands National Park.

TO ENTER CANYONLANDS NATIONAL PARK'S ISLAND IN THE SKY DISTRICT IS TO move into the dead center of the universe and find your place among the spare, unending silences there. The air has a special clarity on this 6,000-foot plateau, which clings to mainland Utah by the slenderest of land bridges. I feel that if I can just get still enough here, the answers to big questions will ride on the thermals to where I sit, tuck themselves into the great pauses between landforms, appear around the next bend in the river.

A mile below, the sinuous Colorado and Green Rivers reach critical mass at their confluence and rage all the way to Lake Powell. The silt-heavy waters of the rivers and their many tributaries have cut deep, meandering lifelines into the rainbow remains of 300-million years of oceans, rivers, shorelines, dune-filled deserts, and braided streams. Here, there are, as Ed Abbey says, "more hills, holes, humps and hollows, reefs, folds, salt domes, swells and grabens, buttes, benches and mesas, synclines, monoclines, and anticlines than you can ever hope to see and explore in one lifetime." But quantity is not the point. The scale of this country is both grand and oddly intimate, terrifying and comforting. The longer I look outward, the more I feel an expansion inside and connect with something greater than myself. The land itself becomes my meditation. I feel at home here.

The rocks of Canyon Country glow with a rich palette of rust-red, salmon pink, light rose, creamy beige, tan, purple, and yellow. Some, such as those of The Needles, are banded. The colors are the result of minerals oxidized from different types of sedimentary rocks by weathering—reds, browns, and yellows come from iron; blue-blacks and purples from manganese. Particularly noticeable are the dark streaks on sandstone slickrock, popularly known as desert varnish. The varnishes are composed of airborne dust and clay particles from dripping water, which are then acted on by bacteria and microfungi. Desert-varnished surfaces at the base of sheer cliffs were irresistible to prehistoric residents, who etched petroglyphs into varnished areas and used hematite (iron-oxide) to paint pictographs on pale expanses of sandstone.

Candlestick Tower, the Maze District, Canyonlands National Park.

Colorful "needles" in Chesler Park, Needles District, Canyonlands National Park.

So have many others. Archaic hunter-gatherers, ancestral Puebloan farmers, modern Utes, Paiutes, and Navajos, cowboys and poets, ranchers and outlaws, miners and uranium prospectors. To the southwest sits the great laccolithic bulk of Navajo Mountain, one of four sacred peaks that enclose the Navajo world and keep it safe. Navajo Mountain and the Henrys, the Cockscomb, the Abajos, the La Sals, the Book Cliffs, and the San Rafael Swell form a circle a hundred miles in diameter around what is now Canyonlands National Park.

From above, the broken landscape seems orderly, like a relief map or perhaps a massive jigsaw puzzle of interlocking rock pieces. Someone else thought so, too, and dubbed The Maze "a thirty-square-mile puzzle in stone," perhaps seeing more confusion than order.

The Chocolate Drops, Maze District, Canyonlands National Park (aerial).

The Great Gallery in Horseshoe Canyon (Barrier Canyon–style pictographs).

Haunted by ghostly rock art and fetishes of the Archaic and ancestral Puebloan cultures, the shades of Butch Cassidy and the Wild Bunch, Mormon polygamists, coyote-wolves and catamounts, The Maze is indeed difficult country to negotiate and survive in. Even to imagine what is there is to connect with our deepest longings, open up our deepest fears. The Needles is equally compelling. An area of salt-collapsed grabens, castellated spires, soft bunch grasses, ancestral Puebloan dwellings, and old cowboy line camps, it lures modern-day explorers willing to lose themselves in its stony embrace.

They all draw me. But on this trip I want to see out, really feel the spaciousness of this country. I spend days walking the headlands of the Island in the Sky to one overlook after another. Upheaval Dome. Mesa Arch. Green River Overlook. Grand View Point. Each place has its own particular slant on things. I drive down long dirt roads outside the park, to destinations known and unknown, waiting for the land to give out.

Anasazi (ancestral Pueblo) ruin, Canyonlands National Park.

Canyon Country was first occupied during the Archaic period by people who hunted and gathered among the canyons and left ghostly pictographs that reveal their unique connections to the natural world. With the introduction of agriculture from Mesoamerica, new farming cultures appeared. Best known were the ancestral Puebloans, who settled southeastern Canyonlands about 1,000 years ago, built rock dwellings and granaries, grew corn, beans, squash, and traded with others, including their neighbors to the west and north, the Fremont. Droughts intensified in the 1200s, and the ancestral Puebloans migrated to better farmlands in present-day New Mexico and Arizona.

Sunrise through Mesa Arch, Island in the Sky District, Canyonlands National Park.

Kangaroo rats, rabbits, canyon mice, and other rodents have little competition in this extreme plateau country. Principal predators are coyotes, the adaptable "song dogs" of the West. Several reptiles, such as the whiptail and the leopard lizard, also do well here, along with gopher snakes and occassionally a rattlesnake. Seldom seen are cougars, which follow herds of deer in remote sections of Arches, and bighorn sheep, the nimble nannies of Canyonlands' White Rim Terrace. Unconstrained by terrain, a variety of birds enjoy the widest access to Canyon Country. Usually present are glossy-feathered ravens, sweetly trilling canyon wrens, a variety of small raptors such as red-tailed hawks and kestrels, and noisy pinyon jays, tits, and other chatty seed eaters.

The Windows area and La Sal Mountains, sunset, Arches National Park.

M Y CONSTANT COMPANIONS DURING MY TRAVELS ARE RAVENS. One morning, at Upheaval Dome, a raven whooshed by, a foot above my head, paused, turned, looked straight into my eyes and croaked, then plunged into the abyss. I shivered although the day was hot.

Another noontime, I sat hidden in my own aerie, high above Mineral Bottom on the Green River, watching three ravens—a mated pair and what seemed to be a juvenile. They performed fly-bys, roll-overs, patrols, and inspections of the territory, their varied creaks and caws rending the torpid silence. Suddenly, one of the birds swooped into a pinyon and seized a little grey bird, possibly a dove or tit, in its talons. It dropped to the ground to deliver the coup de grâce, hungrily pecking at the kill. Outraged, the juvenile began yelling, flapping, and dancing up and down, its screams reverberating down the 1000-foot cliffs for more than an hour. All in vain. The adult did not give up its lunch.

The Colorado River seen from Dead Horse Point, sunrise, Dead Horse Point State Park.

The kill was unusual for a carrion eater but not unknown. Stranger was the witholding of food. According to biologist Bernd Heinrich, mated pairs feed cooperatively and will adopt juveniles and help them hunt. Other youngsters band together and signal each other with yells when they find food, an altruistic behavior with fascinating ramifications. Here, though, the younger bird was apparently being taught a lesson by a dominant adult. Perhaps it was designed to goad the juvenile into fending for itself. Who knows? Survival calls for many strategies, especially when you live in a desert.

Until now, my bird dreams, visions, and close encounters have been filled with eagles. But ravens seem to have something to tell me too, although I'm not yet sure what the message is. It is well known the world over that ravens speak to humans, offer advice, help them find food and win wars. They are considered some of the most intelligent of birds. They are linked with death and evil, but also represent wisdom, prophesy, and the upset in life necessary to create something new. Ravens are shape-shifters, according to Native American lore, and associated with magic, healing, and the spiritual path.

The Green River as it flows through Valentine Bottom, Canyonlands National Park.

The Colorado and Green Rivers and their tributaries are responsible for these dramatically carved canyons. Rising high in the mountains of Colorado and Wyoming, the two rivers run smoothly to their confluence directly below the Island in the Sky, then erupt into whitewater through 14-mile-long Cataract Canyon, and thence to Lake Powell. The rivers have downcut their meanders creating looping goosenecks, which, subject to flashflooding, eventually erode into natural bridges such as those found at Natural Bridges National Monument, south of the Needles. To the southwest lie the Dirty Devil, Fremont, and Escalante rivers. The Escalante was the last river to be named in the United States. It is now part of the new Grand Staircase-Escalante National Monument proclaimed by President Clinton in September, 1996.

Delicate Arch, late afternoon, Arches National Park.

Utah's Arches and Canyonlands National Parks are at the heart of the Colorado Plateau, a dramatic, 130,000-square-mile, uplifted geographical province of the Southwest encompassing portions of Utah, Colorado, Arizona, and New Mexico. Nestled within the Paradox Basin, a low-lying region that was once a vast inland sea, the two parks are celebrated for their remarkable geology and erosional forms. Dominating the horizon on all sides are igneous-intruded peaks, known as laccoliths, which have been stripped of sediments by erosion. Their names were given by early Spanish, Native American, and American travelers and settlers: the La Sals, the Abajos, Navajo Mountain, and the Henrys. The Henrys were the last mountains to be named in the United States.

Raven.

I can live with the mystery of those ravens for a long time. I am glad for the mute presence of the cougar, who I may never see, and the invisible work of bacteria, algae, and lichens in creating new soil so that life can continue. I accept the fate of rivers to surge toward their ocean destiny, transforming everything around them as they go. My pilgrimage may not be so different from those of the ancients who walked deep in the canyons and left their visions for us to ponder. I rejoice in the sublime spectacle of a land that reflects perfect natural order of its own making—a rest from the artifacts of man. "We need wilderness because we are wild animals," insisted Ed Abbey. Among these canyons and formations, the wild has a voice. It sounds like the long echo of spirits calling to one another.

SUGGESTED READING

Abbey, Edward. *DESERT SOLITAIRE: A SEASON IN THE WILDERNESS.* (1968). Reprint. Tucson, AZ: University of Arizona Press. 1988.

Baars, Don. *CANYONLANDS COUNTRY.* Moab, UT: Canyonlands Natural History Association. 1989.

Barnes, F.A. *UTAH CANYON COUNTRY.* Salt Lake City, UT: Utah Geographic Series, Inc. 1986.

Leach, Nicky. *THE GUIDE TO THE NATIONAL PARKS OF THE SOUTH-WEST.* Tucson, AZ: Southwest Parks & Monuments Association. 1992.

Lister, Florence C. and Wilson, Lynn. *WINDOWS OF THE PAST: RUINS OF THE COLORADO PLATEAU.* Mariposa, CA: Sierra Press, Inc. 1993.

Nabhan, Gary Paul and Caroline Wilson. *CANYONS OF COLOR: UTAH'S SLICKROCK WILDLANDS.* San Francisco, CA: Harper Collins West. 1995.

Nicholas, Jeff and Wilson, Lynn & Jim. *ISLANDS IN THE SKY: SCENES FROM THE COLORADO PLATEAU.* Mariposa, CA: Sierra Press, Inc. 1991.

Stegner, Wallace. *BEYOND THE HUNDREDTH MERIDIAN: JOHN WESLEY POWELL AND THE SECOND OPENING OF THE WEST.* (1954). Reprint. New York, NY: Viking Penguin Books. 1992.

Telford, John and Terry Tempest Williams. *COYOTE'S CANYON.* Salt Lake City, UT: Peregrine Smith Books. 1989.

Williams, Terry Tempest. *AN UNSPOKEN HUNGER: STORIES FROM THE FIELD.* New York, NY: Vintage Books. 1994.

PHOTO CREDITS

Willard Clay (Dembinsky Photo Associates): 18
Jack W. Dykinga: 2,12 left
Jeff Gnass: 19 left
George H. Huey: 4
Gary Ladd: 8,9 left,11,22,23,29
J.C. Leacock: 19 right
Mark & Jennifer Miller: 31
Steve Mulligan: 10,12 right,16,17,24 left
William Neill: Front Cover, 7,30
Jeff Nicholas: 14,20,21, Back Cover
Randall K. Roberts: 27
Norm Shrewsbury: 13
William Stone: 24 right, 26
Tom Till: 1,15,25
John Ward: 9 right
Jim Wilson: 28
Eric Wunrow: 5,6

FOR MORE INFORMATION

ARCHES and CANYONLANDS on the INTERNET
www.nps.gov/arch
NATIONAL PARKS INFO ON THE INTERNET
http://www.nps.gov
ARCHES & CANYONLANDS NATIONAL PARKS:
Superintendent, Arches National Park
PO Box 907
Moab, UT 84532
(801) 259-8161
Superintendent, Canyonlands National Park
2282 South West Resource Boulevard
Moab, UT 84532-8000
(801) 259-7164
Canyonlands Natural History Association
3031 South Highway 191
Moab, UT 84532
(801) 259-6003
CAMPGROUND RESERVATIONS (in the parks):
DESTINET, National Park Service Reservations
PO Box 85705
San Diego, CA 92186-5705
(800) 365-CAMP
HOTEL/MOTEL RESERVATIONS (outside the parks):
Utah's Canyonlands Region
PO Box 550-R9
Moab, UT 84532
(800) 635-MOAB or (801) 259-8825
REGIONAL INFORMATION:
Grand Circle Association
PO Drawer HH
Cortez, CO 81321
(800) 253-1616

CREDITS

Book Design: Jeff Nicholas
Editor: Joan Gregory
Photo captions: Nicky Leach
Photo Editor: Jeff Nicholas
Printing coordination: TWP America Inc., Berkeley, CA
Printed in Singapore.

If you would like to receive a complimentary catalog
of our publications, please call:
(800) 745-2631,
or write:
SIERRA PRESS
4988 Gold Leaf Drive, Mariposa, CA 95338